Caroline Charles
1964

Mary Quant
1966

Plate 5

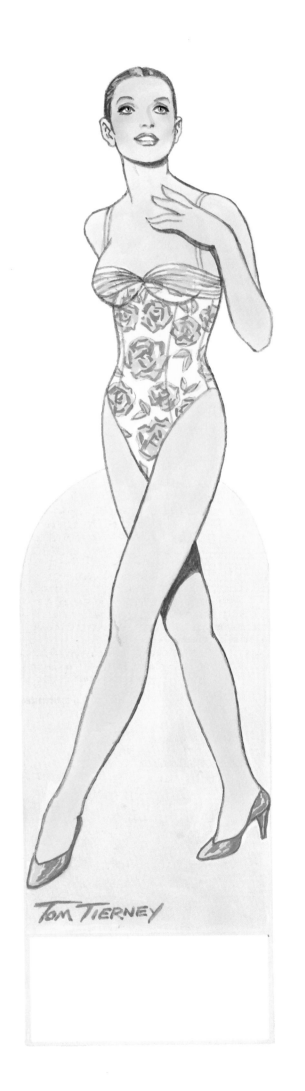

Tom Tierney

Tom Tierney

Plate 1

Do not cut out
white space between
arm and body

Edward Molyneux
1950

Charles Creed
1950

Plate 2

Do not cut out
white space between
arm and body

Sibyl Connolly
1955

Norman Hartnell
1955

Plate 3

Hardy Amies
1956

John Cavanagh
1962

Plate 4

Digby Morton
1967

Barbara Hulanicki
1968

Plate 6

Ossie Clark
1970

Gina Fratini
1970

Plate 7

Do not cut out
white space between
arm and body

Laura Ashley
1970

Jean Muir
1975

Plate 8

Belinda Bellville
1974

Thea Porter
1971

Plate 9

Do not cut out
white space between
arms and bodies

Zandra Rhodes
1977

John Bates
1979

Plate 10

Do not cut out
white space between
arm and body

Bill Gibb
1979

Janice Wainwright
1980

Plate 11

Bruce Oldfield
1984

Betty Jackson
1984

Plate 12

Do not cut out
white space between
arm and body

Georgina Godley
1986

Anthony Price
1986

Plate 13

Do not cut out
white space between
arms and bodies

Katharine Hamnett
1989

Jasper Conran
1990

Plate 14

Do not cut out
white space between
arm and body

John Galliano
1995

Vivienne Westwood
1994

Plate 15

Do not cut out
white space between
arm and body

Rifat Ozbek
1997

Tanya Sarne
1997

Plate 16

* My ~~product~~ garment should be aesthetically and ergonomically be of merchandisable quality. It should be representative of a fine, tailored garment desired to be retailed in an 'up market' couture boutique

* My garment should ~~show~~ find an harmonizing balance between the astrological inspiration and fashionable couture clothing inspiration

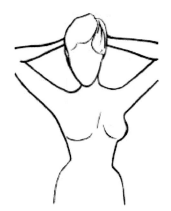